Some people expect that they will be meditating and experiencing exalted states immediately following *kriya* initiation (*diksha*). One attains real meditation, however, only after progressing through a number of lower stages, one of which is *pranayama*.

Without *pranayama,* it is very difficult to withdraw the mind (*pratyahara*) from the senses, to concentrate (*dharana)*, and, through that, to reach meditation (*dhyana*), and finally, *samadhi*. Under the right conditions meditation occurs by itself and is not something that one makes happen. *Kriya pranayam* is the subtle engine that enables this to happen. The correct practice requires the guidance of a *Kriya Guru* who is experienced with this type of *pranayam*.

# Original Kriya Yoga
# Step-by-Step Guide to Salvation
# Volume VI

by Rangin Mukherjee

Copyright 2019

March 12, 2019

Copyright @2019 by Rangin Mukherjee. All rights reserved.

This book or any portion may not be reproduced or used in any manner whatsoever without the express written permission of the publisher with the exception of short quotations used in conjunction with a book review.

First Edition

Rangin Mukherjee
Kolkata INDIA

# Acknowledgements

The following people provided invaluable aid and advice on the compilation and publication of this book:

Mr. Jim Roberts

# Table of Contents

| | |
|---|---|
| *Kriya Lineage* | 9 |
| *Author's Introduction* | 17 |
| *Introduction* | 19 |
| *Questions and Answers* | 27 |
| *Questions from Practitioners* | 57 |
| *A Story about the Kutastha and my Guruji* | 65 |
| *Some Key Points* | 67 |

# Kriya Lineage

Revered Babaji Maharaj
(Khitishwar Maharaj)

The picture of Revered Babaji Maharaj is intentionally left blank. All photos and pictures of Babaji are the result of artistic imagination.

Revered Yogiraj
Lahiri Mahasaya

Shri Nilmadhav Mukhopadhyay
(Swami Pranabananda Paramhangsa)

Param Gurudev
Revered Parmahansa
Pranabananda

# Dedication

To my Guruji's lotus feet

My Gurudev
Revered Gyan Maharaj
(Shri Gyanendranath Mukhopadhyay)

For additional information about the author and his books, visit http://originalkriya.com/. Information about initiation into Original *Kriya Yoga* can be obtained by sending email to kriya.orig@gmail.com.

Here is the current 2019 schedule:

| Dates | Locations | Contact |
| --- | --- | --- |
| Apr 25 – May 23 2019 | Birmingham, England | kriya.orig@gmail.com |
| May 27 – Jun 5 2019 | New Brunswick, NJ USA | kriya.orig@gmail.com |
| Jun 8 – Jun 12 2019 | Los Angeles, CA USA | kriya.orig@gmail.com |
| 3rd week of June 2019 | Seoul, South Korea | bodhilotus@naver.com |

# Author's Introduction

With the completion of this sixth volume of *Original Kriya Yoga,* as well as the previous volume, I would like to say goodbye to all the readers, and to thank you for your encouragement and interest in *Kriya Yoga.* I might have written additional details about meditation and about stabilizing *prana* in *Kutastha,* but my health is not permitting me to write much more. Perhaps God does not want that I should disclose this secret to everyone, but I do promise that by practicing *kriya pranayam* perfectly for a long time, you, yourself, will come to understand this secret on your own, and that one day you will definitely gain *moksha* or salvation.

If you practice the techniques by reading books, you may gain some calmness, but that alone is not enough to progress in *Kriya Yoga.* For that you have to take initiation from a *guru* who can open your third eye during initiation and who can guide you properly on the path of *Kriya Yoga.* The guidance of those *gurus* I see teaching *kriya* is totally wrong. These days I do not see any real *gurus* among them who can open the third eye. There is a famous Sanskrit *sloka* (a couplet of Sanskrit verse) called the *Guru Pranam mantra*:

*Agyana timirandhashya gyananjana shalakaya*
*Chakshurunmilitam yena tasmai shri gurave namah*


It means "You removed the dark blindness of ignorance with the light of supreme knowledge, my salutation to the *guru* who has opened my eyes." So, first, find a *guru* who can open your third eye and guide you properly. Without opening the third eye, you are as a blind in the divine world as a blind person is in the materialistic world. The duty of a <u>true</u> guru is to open the third eye of the disciple and to guide the disciple in the right direction. The duty of the disciple is to follow the *guru* without expectations.

Love to all of you and best wishes for your *kriya* progress.

God bless you.

Sri Mukherjee

# Introduction

Some important stages like birth and death which yogis experience when they are attached to the Almighty are not like that of a normal human being. Although after their birth reborn yogis look a lot like an ordinary baby, they always remain internally attached to the Almighty. They control their own births and deaths.

Nothing can control or depress the yogis about which I am speaking; they live all the time attached to the Almighty and enjoy bliss. At the time of death, they don't become frightened, since at that time their minds remain attached to the Almighty. They never die in unconscious or painful conditions. They leave their body in a joyous condition all the time enjoying the bliss of God.

We will be able to enjoy the above stated stage, when we are able to stabilize our mind in the tunnel of *Kutastha* in *ajna chakra*. There you will find in the center of *Kutastha* a triangular shaped object (*tantra*). It is situated behind, and a little in the upper portion of, the *ajna chakra*. Our soul comes out from the center of the triangle, and everything in this creation comes out through the center of the triangle, spreading all over the universe.

This soul is surrounded by the effects of the three *gunas*: *tamas, rajas*, and *satva*. These three effects are generated from restless *prana* (life force).

When the still mind becomes restless and active, it creates *tamas, rajas*, and *satva* through the three *nadis* (channels) such as *ida, pingala*, and *sushumna*. Thus, blinded or seduced, our undifferentiated soul is covered with joy, sorrow, or illusion (or infatuation) just as a cloud covers the sun.

When *satva guna* becomes active, it gives us certain type of joy with which we become attached, and even sometimes, forget the real joy of life.

When *raja guna* becomes active, it creates desire. We become mad after that desire to fulfill it, thus never allowing ourselves to experience real joy.

When *tamas guna* becomes active, it destroys us and throws us into a dark world. It makes us unenterprising or exhausted, sleepy, and depressed.

According to the movement of breath air, these three effects take place inside our body. Sometimes *satva guna* increases; sometimes *raja guna* increases; and, sometimes *tamas guna* increases. When we breathe through the *ida* channel, *tamas guna* becomes active. When we breathe through *pingala*, *raja guna* becomes active. And, when the breath air remains inside *sushumna*, *satva guna* becomes active.

To be more precise, when the breathing changes its flow from *ida* to *pingala*, or from *pingala* to *ida*, it touches the *sushumna* during the transition.

For example, the movement of breath air not yet completed in *ida*, and the movement of breath air not yet started in *pingala*, that is, in the interim period when breath air stays in *sushumna*. At that time *satva guna* increases. One who can increase the interval of time that the breath air *prana* remains in *sushumna* also increases *satva guna*. Those who are not able to increase that interval, they do mainly the karma of *raja* and *tamas gunas*.

When the soul appears "only in all the senses," it indicates that all the senses have become inactive and that we have become completely absorbed in the soul. It also indicates that *satva guna* has become very active and powerful, and the breath air *prana* moves only through *sushumna* (total stillness).

When *raja guna* increases and becomes active, we tend to perform karma with expectations, and we become very greedy, and also restless. At that time, the breath air *prana* moves through *pingala* which also tends to make us do wrong things, and disturbs us, and so we don't gain any peace at all. In this state, we live always in unrest and turmoil, never gaining peace for a moment.

When the breath air *prana* moves through the *ida* channel, we become idle and exhausted. We do things without judging whether they are proper and logical. At that time most of our decisions prove wrong. We forget our moral duty and perform mostly wrong deeds.

With the increase of *tamas guna* these types of mental changes take place. In other words, mind is guided by the movement of breath air (*pranavayu*) in these three channels such as *ida*, *pingala*, and *sushumna*. Those who do not watch the movement of breath, they do karma according to the *gunas* that are created from the movement of breath air.

But those who watch the breath air according to the Guru's advice, they overcome the restlessness of the breathing; they can hold the *prana* at any place in their body and become free from the three *gunas*.

### At the Time of Death

The most important moment of one's life is at death. This part that I am now describing is about what happens to an advanced *Kriya* yogi at the moment of death. Such a yogi is very active at that time and is not like an ordinary person, perhaps laying around in an unconscious state. This is moment for which we are doing all this *Kriya Yoga* and making so many sacrifices. This is knowing about how to leave the body.

What I am telling you is that at death God gives us a brief moment – a very short period of time -- during which we are free from all diseases and problems. At that time, if you are able to concentrate at the *Kutastha* and chant OM, ascending through the *Brahmarandhra*, you may not have to be reborn. It is that moment which decides your next birth or what happens to you. An advanced *Kriya yogi* like my *Guruji* was able to describe what was happening at the tail end of his life as the *prana* was rising in his body and at what point he would lose the ability to speak.

If a person dies when *satva guna* is increasing during this time, they will live in a clear lighted higher plane where enlightened yogis stay. If a person dies when *raja guna* is increasing during this time, they can't ascend to the higher planes, so they come back to the materialistic world again to take birth in a materialistically-minded family and to perform materialistic work full of expectations. If a person dies during this time when breath air is moving through the *ida* channel, he dies in an unconscious state in total darkness. He will take birth in some lower form.

In short, if we do *satvic* karma, we will see a lighted clear sky and feel happiness. If we do *rajasic* karma, we will get sorrow; and, if we do *tamasic* karma, it will result in a lack of knowledge or ignorance.

When we perform *satvic* karma, *satvic guna* increases, thereby increasing self-knowledge, or wisdom, as the mind increasingly becomes spotlessly clean.

When we perform *rajasic* karma, we get ourselves involved, because of our expectations, with different types of karma (good and bad).

When we perform *tamasic* karma, our ignorance increases over time. With this karma, we lose self-knowledge and wisdom, involving ourselves in different types of evil deeds, etc.

*Satva, raja*, and *tamas gunas* are created from *prana* (life force). The area between *muladhara* and part of the naval area is dominated by *tamas guna* and *raja guna*. The area from the navel area to the throat is dominated by *rajas* and *satva guna* and from the throat to the *ajna chakra* is dominated by *satva guna*. According to the restlessness of *prana*, the position of our mind stays in different *gunas* and we act accordingly.

When mind stays in the area of *satva guna*, our attitude and behavior become very *satvic*. When our mind stays in the *rajas* and *tamas guna* area, our attitude and behavior is very rajasic, fully materialistic; and when our mind stays in *tamas guna*, i.e., *muladhara* to the lower part of navel area, at that time we face sorrow, bindings, infatuations, and mentally face the consequences. When our mind

stays in *raja guna*, at that time we are overwhelmed with successes and egos.

When our mind remains above *satva guna*, it loses its identity. At that time, the mind cannot think of anything; it is beyond our imagination.

A normal human being is always under the influence of the three *gunas: satva, raja,* and *tamas*; and accordingly, he will experience the effects sometimes of happiness, and sometimes of sorrow.

It is only when we reach the stage of no thoughts that the mind becomes totally deactivated, or all functions of mind stop. But it is most difficult to attain that stage because the mind is always dwelling in these three *gunas* and behaves accordingly.

It is only when the mind rises above these three effects that one reaches this stage. It is due to the restlessness of mind that these three *gunas* become active.

When *prana* travels between *ajna chakra* and the navel, i.e., when the *prana* comes down to the navel area, and then becomes still, and does not descend further, it indicates that the *prana* has crossed the stage of *tamas guna*. In other words, one has risen above *tamas guna*.

When the *prana* travels from *ajna chakra* to the throat area, and doesn't descend below the throat area, one has crossed the area of *rajas* and *tamas*. In other words, at this point one has risen above both the *raja* and *tamas gunas*. Here, in this stage, we will experience only *satva guna*.

Finally, when the *prana* does not descend to the throat area, and always remains above the *ajna chakra*, it indicates that one has crossed, or transcended, the effect of all three *gunas* and has reached the stage of thoughtlessness. At this point all three *gunas* remain inside, but one will no longer be attached to the *gunas*.

There are two types of *pranayam*: an outer *pranayam* and inner *pranayam*. The outer *pranayam* occurs when the breath air comes outside the nostrils during *pranayam*. Generally, a human being breathes twelve to fifteen times per minute.

After the completion of one's breathing quota, we leave this world. That means that every minute our life is getting shorter. By the regular practice of perfect *pranayam*, we can convert our outer *pranayam* to an inner *pranayam* during which no breath will leave the nostrils. By practicing inner *pranayam* for a long time, we can get rid of our desires.

# Questions and Answers

**What is *Kriya Yoga* and why should we practice *kriya*?**

*Kriya Yoga* is a spiritual science by which an individual soul becomes merged into the Universal Soul. The Universal Soul is another way to describe the Absolute. By merging into the Absolute, we can become free from the cycles of birth and death. So, we should practice *kriya* to eliminate birth and death forever.

**What are *moksha* (mokhs) and salvation? And what are their differences?**

In *moksha*, we remain with God in one of five different levels. The five types of *moksha* mentioned in Volume II are *shalokyo*, *shamipyo*, *sharupa*, *shasti*, and *shajuyo*.

In salvation, we ourselves become dissolved with the Almighty. That is, we become Almighty. For example, when a water flows over land, we called it a river; and when the same water is mixed with the ocean, we call it the ocean and no longer refer to it as a river. So, when it is mixed with it, the water that makes up the river becomes the ocean. When individual soul is mixed with the Universal Soul, we ourselves become the Almighty.

Countless words have been written with only limited success in order to explain in what way, and to one degree, one becomes One with God or the Almighty. Without first achieving realization, it is far better to spend one's time sincerely practicing rather to try to understand in detail the final end-state of becoming dissolved in the Almighty.

This brings to mind the difficulty of even trying to explain *Kriya*. What is understandable at one level of consciousness may not be understandable at another. What is true at one level may not be true at another. When we have no experience in a subject matter and attempt to understand what is currently beyond our ken [range of awareness], the ideas we form about it may not be accurate and can mislead us.

Topics like *uttam pranayam* and internal breathing are difficult to explain. I have given here an introductory idea about how these things work. As your practice advances, you will be able to understand these things on your own.

**What is the difference between God and the Almighty?**

We can see God after piercing the *ajna chakra*. So long as duality exists, God has form and can be described, but the Almighty is formless and cannot be described. Only joy exist there. The Almighty is endless. We become absorbed with the Almighty to gain salvation.

**What are the techniques to gain *moksha* or salvation?**

After getting initiation, our first task is to maintain the *yamas* and *niyamas*. (The rules of "right living.")

Then, we have to practice *pranayam* perfectly for a long period of time until our *asana* becomes firm without any movement, and we can sit still for a long time, while our mind is fixed in *ajna chakra*, and our breathing is subtle and long.

*Pranayam* represents a very restless period. During this time, any vision that comes, comes only for the briefest time --- mere seconds until we enter the *sushumna nadi*. It is then that the second *kriya* starts.

At that time, we have to use force on *pranayam* and force our *prana* to enter different channels (*nadis*). In this way, we control different places in our body. Sometimes we use force on *prana*; and sometimes, we hold the *prana* in different places in our body.

As mentioned in earlier volumes, self-realization occurs in the *Kutastha*. After piercing the *ajna chakra*, we practice the second stage of meditation (*dharana*) followed by the third stage of meditation (*dhyana*) which leads us to *samadhi*, and, finally, to *moksha* and salvation.

**How do we calm our mind?**

We can calm our mind by eating *satvic* foods, reading spiritual books, thinking spiritually, and, in general, by overall practicing correct *pranayam* strictly according to the instructions we receive in initiation. This includes eating only vegetarian items, and especially, it includes avoiding eggs, or any products that contains eggs.

We should avoid jealousy, anger, gossip about others, as well as other negative attitudes or displays of behavior; instead, we should think wellness and good thoughts for all. We should help people in distress and try to live without any attachments and obsessions. These things help calm our mind.

**What is the difference between calmness and restlessness?**

When our mind becomes totally desireless, nothing will disturb our mind, even when we find ourselves in very disturbing situations.

In a few words, the mind becomes indifferent to everything existing in this world and remains completely uninterested.

Restlessness occurs when our *prana*, or breathing, becomes uneven. Then, desires for everything will increase; and, we are never satisfied with what we have. Consider the restlessness of a monkey. They can't remain in one place for long, always searching for something. With restlessness of mind, one cannot concentrate properly; and so, with a restless mind, one will never be able to practice *pranayam* correctly.

**Why is our aim in *Kriya Yoga* to gain calmness?**

Without calmness of our mind, it is impossible to concentrate properly. Without calmness, no progress in *kriya* can occur. It is like a pond. When the pond is calm, we can see the reflection of the moon very clearly. But if the pond is not still, we won't see any reflection of the moon. It is the same with the vision of God which requires calmness.

**How can we progress faster in *Kriya Yoga*?**

In order to progress faster, one must first master perfect *pranayam*. This step must take place first before one can progress, as each step builds on the previous step.

And in order to practice perfect *pranayam*, we need to follow strictly *yama* and *niyama* [all the rules of "right living"].

In the lower six *chakras*, perfect *pranayama* is the main practice. Performing *pranayam*, and watching the sixth chakra, simultaneously is called perfect *pranayam*. After we enter *sahasrara*, *pranayama* is no longer required.

**What is the difference between materialistic enjoyments and divine enjoyments?**

Materialistic enjoyments are temporary and create sorrow. These enjoyments are not good for spiritual practices as well as for one's health. A person who is addicted to materialistic enjoyment can never progress on the spiritual path.

The result is that one faces endless births and deaths. We will never attain *moksha* until we give up the materialistic life.

Divine enjoyment is totally different. It occurs internally and permanently. One can enjoy it 24x7 for the rest of his life. It is also endless enjoyment and cannot be expressed. One can get no such joy in the materialistic world. This enjoyment happens with great satisfaction.

**What are the *chakras* and their functions?**

*Chakras* are a bunch of outgoing and incoming nerve plexuses connected with the brain, especially with the Area of Intellect and with the ten *indriyas* (senses). [The *indriyas* are composed of five *jnanendriyas* and five *karmendriyas*].

### Why is food so important for *kriya* practitioners?

There are three types of food each of which has with a different effect upon us:

- *Satvic* foods – This includes generally all types of fruits and vegetables.
- *Rajasic* foods – This includes eggs and all types of meat, including onions and garlic, and muscular pulses, like masoor dal (spiced red lentils).
- *Tamasic* foods – This includes old stale foods, food or drink that is too hot or too cold, too much alcohol, etc.

Here are their effects:

- With *satvic* foods, the mind becomes calm, concentration increases, the food is digested easily; and it is also good for health.
- With *rajasic* foods, the mind becomes restless, and concentration decreases. The veil over the inner world increases, and visions in the inner world take place less often.
- With *tamasic* foods, the mind creates jealous, anger, and harmful attitudes. It becomes impossible to concentrate. One is without vision, as nothing appears, and one sees only darkness.

### How do the effects of these foods take place?

After eating food, it is transported to our stomach where it is further grinded, and portions of it are converted into a white juice like milk which is absorbed by certain channels and then mixed with the blood. Thus, we get nutrients from the effects of foods we intake.

Just as nutrients do, different types of food have different types of effects on our mind as stated above.

### What the signs of progress in *Kriya Yoga*?

After practicing *Kriya Yoga* for some time, some signs of progress begin to manifest, depending on how perfectly we are practicing *pranayam*. Below progress is described serially one after another, although the same ordering may not always be noticed by the practitioner.

- At first the sitting posture will be perfect.
- Breathing will become longer and smoother.
- The mind starts watching the sixth *chakra* for longer periods of time. One starts to experience a type of satisfaction.
- The mind will become calm.
- The internal sky becomes clearer.
- A type of sparkling of light appears from time to time.
- Some types of vision start appearing only for a very brief time (perhaps only a second).
- Interest in *kriya* practice will increase.
- A type of happiness will start.
- Breathing will start becoming subtle.
- Force on *pranayam* will start increasing.
- The practitioner will gradually lose interest in leading a materialistic life.
- The mind can be fixed in *ajna chakra* for longer periods of time.
- Increased happiness will start along with high satisfaction.
- The mind enters *sushumna nadi*.

After this, the practice of the second *kriya* begins.

**Why should we concentrate on *Kutastha*?**

All our nerves connect at *Kutastha*. It is the source of *prana*. If someone gets injured by accident at that place, one may die instantly, since it is the main source of *prana*. All our divine experiences happen here.

It is the borderline of *Karma Yoga* (Area of Action) and *Bhakti Yoga* (Area of Devotion). It is lying on the backside of the *ajna chakra*. It is the place where we meet God.

**What is OM? And why should we chant OM in *pranayama*?**

OM is the language of God and the Almighty. Without chanting OM, if we practice *pranayama*, i.e. only inhaling and exhaling, then we will be performing only a breathing exercise.

**What is the route of *sushumna*?**

Some organizations teach *Kriya Yoga* saying that one should imagine *prana* going up and down the spinal cord, as one inhales and exhales. In *Kriya Yoga* imagining has no place. In yoga we have to get direct knowledge and so there is no place for imagination.

If we understand the route of *sushumna* clearly, then we can understand the truth of how *kriya* works. Whatever vision that we experience, it is always through the *ajna chakra*. *Prana* travels through the *sushumna*, that is, inside *sushumna*. The open end of *sushumna* is connected to *ajna chakra*. It is the meeting place of *sushumna*, i*da*, and *pingala*.

It is only through the *ajna chakra* that we discover that the *sushumna* is connected with all other *chakras*. If *ajna chakra* were not connected with them, and if the connecting route to all of them did not occur through the *sushumna*, we would not experience the knowledge we obtain from all the lower *chakras*.

**What is the difference between our breath and *prana*?**

Breath air, which we can feel while breathing, is grosser than *prana*, but inside our body, *prana* is the force which causes us to exhale and inhale. In a few words, *prana* is the subtle form of breathing and works like a pump.

**What is the best time to practice *kriya*?**

The actual best time to practice *kriya* is from 9:30pm to 4:30am. Since it is not possible for everyone to practice this way; alternatively, in the beginning, one practices, every day in the mornings from 4am to 6am, and in the evenings from 6pm to 8pm is all right. Later on, 3am to 6am and 6pm to 9pm, making a total 6 hours.

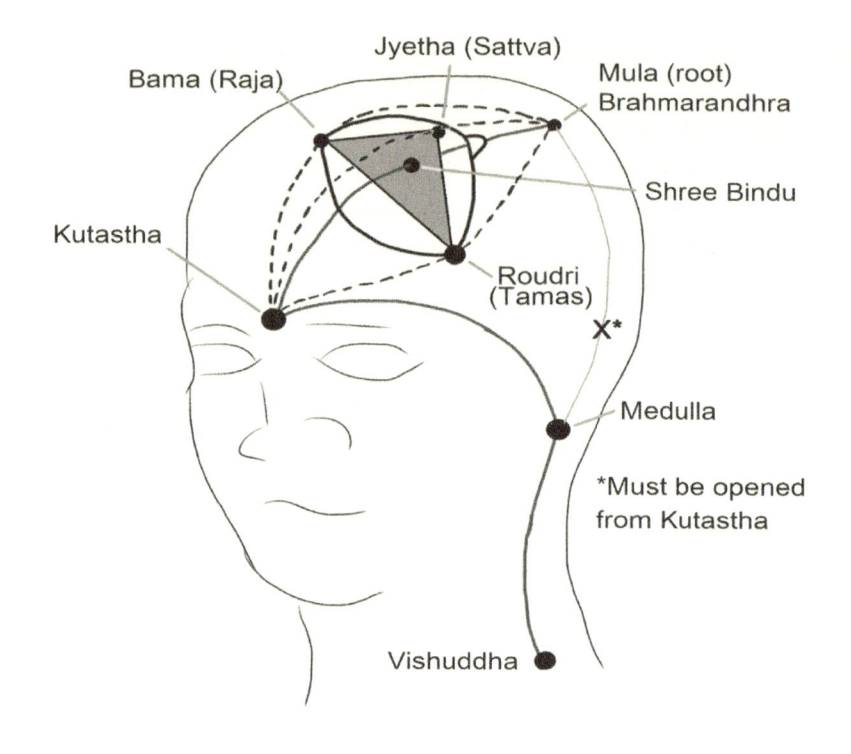

*Illustrating the Proper Route to Brahmarandhra*

The previous volume (V) described the proper route that a *kriya* practitioner takes to reach *brahmarandhra*.

To review briefly:

> "After traversing the lower *chakras*, the *sushumna* then enters the head through two different routes. One route goes up to the *brahmarandhra* from the medulla where the *mula chakra* is located with its end closed. ...
>
> Since this ... end is closed and it has no connection with this end of the *sushumna*, it opens only when, from the open end, the force of *prana* is applied; otherwise, it remains closed. Thus, we have to ascend through the *ajna chakra* and not through the closed end that is connected to *mula*."

In order to make this easier to understand, the accompanying sketch illustrates the routes.

**In the beginning of our practice, why shouldn't we use force on *pranayama*?**

At the beginning of our practice, our nerves are blocked with bile (*pitta*), phlegm (*kapha*), and wind or air (*vata*). Now, if we use force aiming to clean the nerves, the force of *prana* will create pressure inside the nerves; and this pressure will create a distortion of the *prana*, instead of distributing *prana* to all the nerves of our body. So, if we use force in the beginning of our practice, our nervous systems will be distorted. There is also a chance that our health will ultimately break down and that we could get chest pains, headaches, etc.

Our first step is to clean the nerves. This process is called *nadi shuddhi*. The best way to start this process is to practice *pranayam* using our normal breathing. At this stage one should never use force. It is only after achieving subtle *pranayam* that we should use force on *pranayam*.

By practicing correct *pranayam* for a long time, gradually all our nerves inside our body calm down. Finally, after the cleaning of *ida* and *pingala*, *sushumna* at last gets cleaned. At this point, we will be eligible to begin the second *kriya* in which we have to use force during *pranayam*, then drive our *prana* through different cleaned channels to different places inside our body, and finally fix or stabilize our *prana* in *ajna chakra*.

### What is kundalini?

*Kundalini* is the cosmic power that remains in a dormant state for most people and is coiled up in the lowest part of the spinal cord. *Kundalini* gets activated when our mind and *prana* enter the *swadhisthana chakra*. Then *brahma nadi* which is inside *sushumna* and goes up through *bajra* [*vajra*] and *chitra nadi* (described in previous volume) pierces all the lotuses. When we enter *vajra (bajra) nadi*, we lose the sense of the outer world. Of these, the *brahma nadi* is the subtlest.

It is called the activation of *kundalini* power when mind enters this *nadi*. It creates pure intelligence. Whatever a *kriya* practitioner wants to know, he will be able to know everything. That is why is also called the *nadi* of knowledge. One end of this *Brahma nadi* is in *muladhara* which is open. The other end is in *sahasrara* which is closed. At the time of death, all realized yogis open the closed end in *sahasrara chakra* by coming from the *ajna chakra* and leave the body, thus obtaining salvation.

**What should a yogi do at the time of death?**

A yogi should drive the *prana* through *sushumna* from *ajna chakra* to *mula chakra* (not *muladhara chakra*) in *sahasrara* where both ends of *sushumna* meet and should use force from the open end of *sushumna* to the closed end of the other part of *sushumna*.

Thus, by opening the curtain of the other part of *sushumna*, and then by joining the both ends of *sushumna*, a yogi can achieve salvation. (This can be known through direct *guru's* mouth.)

For others they should watch *ajna chakra* and should mentally chant OM. This way one can get *moksha* or at least will enter paradise. If he gets *moksha*, he can stay at those plans as long as he wants and then come back to this world to practice *Kriya Yoga* and complete this technique.

**If we don't attain *moksha* or salvation in this life, does that mean that all our efforts and sacrifice have all been in vain?**

No, not at all. If we do not attain it in this life, then we will come back to *Kriya* in the next life, reaching very quickly the same state that we managed to complete in this life. From that point on, the rest of the path, we have to complete in the usual way until we attain salvation.

All our genuine efforts and sacrifices will never be in vain. That is why without wasting any more time, we must start practicing *kriya* immediately. In the case of those practicing fake *kriya*, those efforts will be totally wasted.

In the case of practicing the original *kriya* of Lahiri Mahasaya, this *kriya* we will get automatically so long we will take birth and until we get salvation. This is the wonder of original *Kriya Yoga*.

**What is the difference between normal breathing and** *pranayama*?

In normal breathing, we breath haphazardly, that is, sometimes long, sometimes short, sometimes with force, sometimes without force, sometimes fast, and sometimes slow, without chanting any sacred word.

During the practice of *pranayam*, the first thing we have to do is to concentrate between our eyebrows, that is, we watch the centre of our eyebrows with our mind without stressing our eyes.

And with the inhalation and exhalation of our breath, we have to chant OM. Without OM, it will simply be a breathing exercise that won't help us to keep our mind calm. This is also called rhythmic breathing.

**Why is** *pranayam* **so important in** *Kriya Yoga*?

*Pranayam* is the only technique to calm the mind. There is no other way. We cannot do real meditation without practicing *pranayam*. Deep meditation only begins after piercing the *ajna chakra*.

From the muladhara to the *ajna chakra*, we practice *pranayam* making the mind calm from its restless stage.

**Why is initiation required?**

Only through initiation is our third eye opened. Just as without our two eyes, we are blind in the materialistic world, in the divine spiritual world, we are blind without the spiritual or third eye. A *guru* should have the power to open the third eye. Practicing *Kriya Yoga* without opening the third eye is of no value as we will not be able to see the divine spiritual world.

## What is fake *Kriya*? What is the result of practicing fake *Kriya*?

Fake *kriya* is the inauthentic teaching of the original *kriya*. It was created due to the mistaken understanding of Lahiri Mahasaya's *kriya* teachings by some so-called *kriya gurus*. The end result of practicing fake *kriya* for its practitioners is zero development, wasted time, and the creation of enormous frustration and disbelief.

The difference between the two types of *kriya* is simple: one *kriya* is authentic, and the other is not *kriya* at all, but merely *kriya* only in name. How can this be known?

Dear Reader, please consider that already in print there are a number of so-called 'tell-all books' about *Kriya Yoga* that purport to reveal everything one would want to know about *Kriya*. In my books, I have discussed things not discussed in these other books or in organizations that teach *Kriya*.

Just to site a few examples: the huge role of *pranayam* and the *Kutastha* that was emphasized by Yogiraj Lahiri Mahasaya, but is not properly addressed in other teachings about *kriya,* various kinds of *pranayam*: *uttam, antarmukhi pranayam, chaturthik* (described elsewhere), *sthira vayu* (subtle breath), the lighting up of one's inner sky, the real meaning of offering the incoming breath to the outgoing breath and vice-versa, piercing the *chakras*, the proper route to *brahmarandhra*, a description of how *Patanjali's* eight steps are part and parcel of *Kriya Yoga*.

The point is not about any one of these things alone, but they from a part of what one experiences and practices in the course of the long and patient practice of *Kriya* Yoga that one does in order to be successful. If those teaching and writing about *Kriya* understood the process from experience, don't you think it is likely that they would be writing something about it, especially since they aim to tell all? In other words, what are the steps that a *kriya* yogi experiences in the course of his development?

Since they do not speak from actual experience, you can draw your own conclusions. I have written enough for those who take initiation to get started and to progress on the *kriya* path. You won't obtain an understanding of how it works from these other teachings.

*Pranayam* is the main weapon to make our minds calm from its restless stage. If the practice of *pranayam* is wrong, no progress will be achieved, even if someone were to practice the wrong method for a thousand years. As I have said several times, practicing *pranayam* and imagining that the *prana* is moving inside the spinal cord is a totally wrong practice. It is simply a waste of time.

**What is subtle *pranayam* and how does one get it?**

After practicing *pranayam* for some time, we will notice that our breath is becoming smoother and longer. We will start enjoying a type of comfort while doing *pranayama*.

We will not feel breath air outside of our nostrils. Everything will happen inside our bodies, and we will not feel like breathing, even though we do *pranayam* with force. A type of satisfaction persists.

The mind starts getting fixed in *ajna chakra*. Calmness of mind begins. This is the starting point of subtle *pranayam*.

**Should a *kriya* practitioner establish an ashram?**

One should never establish an ashram. Lahiri Mahasaya never encouraged the establishment of ashrams. Creating an ashram runs completely counter to his wishes. There are lots of negative aspects in establishing an ashram. Today the original *Kriya Yoga* became fake *Kriya Yoga* because of ashram people.

It is true that at an early point in his teaching of *Kriya Yoga*, Swami Pranabananda established in ashram. This ashram was located in the same neighborhood where Lahiri Mahasaya lived. Later on, Swami Pranabananda renounced an ashram that he might have inherited and whose endowment would have afforded him a comfortable lifestyle; after that experience, he steadfastly refused all efforts to entangle him in the establishment of an ashram.

It has been said that ashrams encourage a begging mentality and an institutional egoism. On rare occasions an ashram has spontaneously arisen around a realized person (like Ramana Maharishi) by others to support their *sadhana* without the realized person's making any effort. In this case, the realized person will not involve themselves in soliciting donations for land, buildings, or food. When this happens, whatever support that comes to the ashram, comes of itself. Ashrams eventually entangle its inhabitants in *maya*.

The builders of *Kriya* ashrams have spoiled the originality of *Kriya Yoga* and also spoil the life of so many genuine *kriya* seekers. They are teaching what they have understood about *kriya* practice, but unfortunately have missed its essence. That way the original *kriya* has become fake *kriya*.

Parmahansa Yogananda began practicing *Kriya Yoga* at an early age in his youth, but later on in America he became mired in the organizational life of supporting an ashram. Also, at some point, perhaps in the ashram environment of his *guru*, the focus and emphasis in teaching *Kriya Yoga* shifted, from focusing solely on the *Kutastha* during *pranayam,* and morphed to focusing on the more conceptual and "scientific-sounding" approach preferred by his *guru* of spinal breathing. Regardless of this, Yogananda still knew that focusing on the *Kutastha* was crucial, as this snippet citing him from the internet shows:

"Sir, is there a scientific method, apart from Kriya Yoga, that will lead a devotee to God?" a student inquired.

"Yes," the Master said. "A sure and swift way to the Infinite is to keep one's attention at the Christ (Kutastha) center between the eyebrows."

In *Kriya Yoga*, we experience everything directly. There is no place for imagining every experience we receive from the *Kutastha*. So, watch and concentrate deeply in *Kutastha* and no other place in the body.

**Should we maintain secrecy in *Kriya Yoga*?**

Of course. We have to practice *kriya* very secretly behind closed doors and should not tell anyone about our experiences while practicing *kriya*.

We may only discuss it with our *guru* or, when appropriate, with our spiritual brothers; otherwise, it will create ego.

### Is it all right to have many friends?

Always try to avoid too much social activity with friends, especially those who do not believe in God or *kriya*. Too much gossiping is not good.

**Understand that while you are immortal, your body is not, and that one day it be destroyed.**

We have to watch the *Kutastha* always with our mind and not try to see within using our physical eyes. The inner (spiritual) eye will automatically follow our mind. Suppose you open your eyes and concentrate on any object in a room. Then your *whole* attention is with your mind. If you just watch with your eyes, your mind will no longer be there; it will be elsewhere. With these physical eyes you can see only the material (physical) world. So, watch the *Kutastha* keeping your attention only there.

### How much sleep is enough?

Six hours sleep is enough for a practicing yogi doing *kriya*. Those working in hard labor may require eight hours; those working without hard labor may require less. As you advance along the *kriya* path, you will require less.

My guru used to sleep only two-three hours per night (in twenty-four hours). He was always cheerful and lived to the age of 103. He needed less sleep because he could relax in deep meditation.

At the beginning of your practice, if you sleep too little or too much, you will not be able to concentrate properly. So be realistic and find the right balance for where you are at this point in your *sadhana*.

**Should we take a cold bath in the morning?**

If you live in a place that not have much heating (so your water is cold), you should not take a bath/shower very early in the morning.

**Is there a need also to do pujas?**

There is no need to do other pujas if we practice *kriya* regularly. *Kriya Yoga* provides *Brahma Veda* (knowledge of Brahma). Up and until *ajna chakra*, one is still in duality. When you are doing *Kriya Yoga*, you are doing *puja* inside your body. Everything is there. When you reach the second *kriya* you will see all your idols within.

**What is divine intoxication and when does it occur?**

Divine intoxication is a type of intoxication that happens generally after *kriya pranayam* or after *paravasta*. During divine intoxication, the mind becomes thoughtless. A type of trance comes. The head becomes heavy; and we will not feel like talking, or hearing anything, or opening the eyes.

One stays totally dumb similar to the effects after smoking marijuana (which interferes with concentration). After little progress in *kriya*, this intoxication becomes more intense and deeper. The difference is that with divine intoxication we feel a kind of joy. We will feel not hungry or thirsty; and a type of satisfaction and comfort will be felt.

**What is *uttam pranayam*?**

It was already mentioned in previous volumes about the three stages of *pranayam*: first, second, and third stage.

This third stage of *pranayam* is called *uttam pranayam*, which is also highest stage of *pranayam*. By practicing the first and second stage of *pranayam*, we reach the stage of *uttam pranayam*.

It takes 40 to 44 seconds to complete one inhalation and one exhalation. Breathing becomes extremely subtle and automatically forceful. No breath air will be felt outside the nostrils. The whole *pranayam* process will be inside our body. This is also called *antarmukhi pranayam* or internal *pranayam*.

*Pranayam* is to be done in the *shat chakras,* i.e. inside *sushumna* in the six *chakras*. With *uttam pranayam* we have to pierce all the lower chakras. It makes a sound like a flute. That is why by practicing the *pranayam* which we get from our *guru* in the initial stage that we can eventually achieve *uttam pranayam* (3rd stage). Only with long practice of proper *pranayam* can we achieve *uttam pranayam*. To achieve that, we need to practice *pranayam* according to the guru's instructions for a long time with patience. If we lose patience, nothing can be achieved.

By practicing *uttam pranayam* 12 times, we reach *pratyahara*. By practicing it for $12 \times 12 = 144$ times, we get *dharana* (meditation 2nd stage), and by practicing it for $144 \times 12 = 1728$ times, we get *dhyana* (meditation 3rd stage).

At this point, we gain a permanent type of happiness. Ordinary happiness is of no consequence and makes no difference. Nothing can disturb our mind as it becomes indifferent to everything. Then, by practicing 1728x12 = 20736 in one sitting, we get *samadhi*.

Then we have to try to stay in *samadhi* for a longer period of time so that the *samadhi* becomes deeper. At this stage we will be able to control all our senses. With the help of *uttam pranayam* our body and mind get purified, i.e., both body and mind become still or fixed.

In the beginning of our practice, we should try to make our body and mind motionless. At that stage there will be no restrictions about *asana, yamas*, and *niyamas*.

Everything will happen automatically with this *pranayam*, only we have to sit in a comfortable posture.

Then we have to stabilize the *kundalini* power in *Kutastha* with the help of *sthira vayu*, i.e., translated exactly as 'fixed air' or sometimes called the tranquil breath (sometimes it is very difficult to express all these terms in English). (As I wrote in an earlier volume, the addiction to the tranquil breath is so great that the mind can be occupied with the desire to practice *pranayam* twenty-four hours a day. Doing perfect *pranayam* with the tranquil breath brings indescribable joy.)

Then a type or argument and confusion can start mentally. What I see, has anyone else seen these visions? All these visions real?

A type of *samadhi* happens that is called *savitarka samadhi*. This comes under the classification of *samprajnata samadhi* or the first stage of *samadhi*. In *samprajnata samadhi* our mind and *prana* become fixed, no deflection happens, but the sense of self existence is there, and also understanding of different stages of our existence.

The inner or subtle world again divide into four different stages like reasoning (*vitarka*), reflection (*vichara*), joy (*ananda*), and egotism (*asmita*) in four different places like mind (*manas*), intellect (*buddhi*), ego (*ahamkara*) and *chitta* (storehouse of thoughts) and when everything disappears, no sense or knowledge exists. This is called *asamprajnata samadhi* or *chaitanya samadhi* which is our target.

Therefore, we have to practice *pranayam* daily as much as possible to first reach *uttam pranayam* which requires lots of time to reach. After we achieve *uttam pranayam*, we become able to enter the *sushumna*, i.e., start the second *kriya* that we do only with *uttam pranayam*.

So long we breathe through *ida* and *pingala*, our quota of breath becomes less and less, since breath air goes out through the nostrils. We can say that it is due to the outward flow of the breath air.

But in *sushumna* the tendency of the breath air to exit out the nostrils stops and the *apana* goes up to *ajna chakra* and stabilizes there. This is called the upward movement of *apana*. At the time of death if we can leave our body through *sushumna*, we may not have to take birth again.

By practicing *uttam pranayam*, when our *prana* becomes still, our mind also becomes still. That still mind is our soul. Therefore, we have to fix our mind in *ajna chakra* and never allow our mind to come down. In this way we may control all our *indriyas* (senses).

**How long should it take to complete one *uttam pranayam*?**

One *uttam pranayam* takes 40 to 45 seconds generally. In the beginning of learning *kriya*, we feel the breath flowing out through our nostrils. When we are in a normal state, relaxed, and practicing, you may notice sometimes that the breath may extend to a length of 12 fingers. When the breath becomes subtler and subtler, its length will gradually become less and less, until one day no breath is coming out, but you are still breathing. This seems impossible, but such is the inner or *uttam pranayam*. At first, the shock of this may cause one to bring his forefinger up to the nostrils to verify this.

Yogis say that if one were able to measure it, the full length of the *uttam pranayam* would be a minimum of 22 fingers. This is very close to the length of the spinal column (45cm or almost 18 inches). In *uttam pranayam*, you are still breathing, but not in the way that would normally breath. This is a sign you are entering the inner world.

Now, this is important, when you practice *uttam pranayam* in *sushumna (*as the second *kriya*), you are using mental force, but <u>even with that force you are not feeling any breath air</u>! You feel the force inside, but nothing outside, as you pierce the *chakras* one at a time.

It is a very difficult period when you start the second *kriya*. It is a dangerous period because you will face all sorts of obstructions. You have to possess tremendous mental strength because the temptations (sexual and other) are so great. Things that you think you have overcome will come back to attack you, until you have pierced the *manipura chakra*.

**When can we increase the number of *pranayams*?**

In the beginning we should practice 108 *pranayams* twice every day before sunrise and after sunset. In the case of retired persons, practice three times a day. Always try to practice two times a day (minimum).

After a little advancement, we may practice *pranayam* 108 times in the morning (which will always be fixed); and in the evening, we may increase the count gradually to 308 times. To increase gradually, one may increment the total count by 10 *pranayams* every 15 days.

Once one reaches a new count, it is important to commit internally to practice this same number every day. As a result, one would never end up practicing 308 pranayams one day, 108 the next, and 208 the following day. Regularity in practice is important!

As Lahiri Mahasaya taught, it is better to do two perfect *pranayams* than to do 200 *pranayams* haphazardly.

Always try to practice two times a day (minimum). It is only 108 *pranayam* every day in the morning time, but you can gradually increase the number of *pranayam* in the evening.

### When should we practice meditation or *paravasta*?

Meditation or *paravasta* mean the same thing. After *kriya* we have to increase gradually the time we spend in meditation and should to remain longer in calmness. Thus, gradually we will enter the stage of *dharana* and thereafter *dhyana* and *samadhi*.

After finishing our *kriya* and *mudras* we have to start meditation. Since *pranayam* and *mudras* are restless stages, and meditation is totally a calm stage, when we start meditating, it becomes very difficult to fix our mind in *ajna chakra*. Your mind will start telling you to stop for now and to concentrate another day. It is the mind that tries to disturb us. But we should not listen to the mind and keep concentrating.

After practicing *kriya pranayam*, it is good to spend at least an hour every time practicing meditation. In meditation, there are no limits as to how long we can practice. Real meditation provides a deep rest and is much more relaxing so that you won't have to sleep as long once you reach that stage. In *samadhi*, you are not dreaming, but getting spiritual knowledge.

**What is *antarmukhi pranayam* (or internal *pranayam*)?**

Internal pranayam will happen after our breathing becomes very subtle. Internal pranayam means, the entire breathing takes place inside our body, i.e. no breath air will come out from our nostrils. This may seem impossible, until it occurs. At that time, mainly our *prana* (life force) will be active. It will not have any connection with the breath air, which is gross. In other words, we are proceeding towards subtle world from the gross world.

**What are the *granthis* (knots)?**

There are three *granthis* (knots in the *sushumna*) which are called Brahma, Vishnu, and Rudra *Granthi*. They are all pierced by practicing perfect *pranayam*. So, our duty is to practice perfect *pranayam*. Other things will happen automatically.

**How does one stop rebirth?**

There are many theories about how one might stop rebirth so as not to have to be reborn. Depending on our level of development, all these might be correct.

Here is another technique to gain salvation. When a piece of coal gets heated thorough a coal-fired furnace, the piece of coal at first becomes reddish. Then it turns into a bluish color; and finally, with the addition of more heat, it becomes whitish. This whitish color appears.

At the time of death, we don't have to do *pranayam*, it happens automatically and is called *chaturthik pranayam*. At that time, we watch the spot (the *ajna chakra*) as per our *Guru's* advice and apply *thokar* (force) to leave this body and to gain salvation. It is the highest stage of death. Those who see only darkness at the time of death, they take birth again and again.

**In the midst of all our activities, how is it possible to be attached to God all the time?**

Suppose you are riding on a bicycle. At the same time, you are also balancing on the bicycle, perhaps speaking with your friend and navigating your surroundings as you ride, all the while you do this while maintaining your balance. In the same way, you can be working a job while maintaining your contact with God.

Another example, in Rajasthan you will sometimes see women, as they walk along the road, carrying several pots of water on their head while also chatting and gossiping with each other. So, likewise you are able to do all sorts of things at the same time as keeping an awareness of God. The mind can be in different places at the same time.

**Is it a sin to change *guru*?**

We can only change *guru* if we don't get any results after sincere practice of *kriya yoga* for one or two years.

### What is *Sharanga Yoga*?

By practicing *pranayam* for a long time when our *prana* comes to a standstill, i.e., endless *Brahma* Almighty appears. This is also the endless form of *Prana*. At that stage there is a different kind of *shat chakra*, i.e. *kriya* of the six *chakras* that can be done. This kriya of *shatchakra* is called *Sharanga Yoga*. It has to be practiced per the *guru*'s advice.

### What is *yugta abastha* or being completely connected with Brahma (Almighty)?

When the mind comes to a total standstill, at that time the individual soul is connected with the universal soul. All the functions of the body will be stopped. No desires and expectations will arise in the mind. This is called *yukta abastha*.

When a kriya practitioner becomes thoughtless and becomes totally still and can see (view) himself (his soul), he realizes his actual identity just above the *ajna chakra* in *Tatpada* which only a real *guru* can show his disciples while opening the third eye at the time of initiation. In the center of *Tatpada* is the *bindu* (*Brahmari Guha*) upon which we concentrate. Without opening the third eye, it is not a real initiation and so the initiation will be fruitless.

Therefore, initiation from a *guru* has to be taken who can open the third eye, applying the power of his lineage *gurus*, and guide the disciple in the right direction.

Even a person who has committed endless sins may get *moksha* or salvation if he changes his character and starts practicing very sincerely *kriya pranayam*. By practicing perfect kriya *pranayama* all our sins will be washed out. So, don't worry about the past. Just change your lifestyle and start practicing *kriya* immediately without further wasting your time.

To progress in *Kriya Yoga* both our body and mind has to be pure. By taking *satvic* foods and living *satvic* life, we can have a pure body. Also limited exercise, quantity of foods, and sleep makes our body pure. Thus, practicing *pranayama, pratyahara, dharana, dhyana*, and *samadhi* makes our mind pure. An impure body and mind are a sin. *Rajas* and *tamas gunas* are dirt of mind and body.

So long as we have a dirty body and mind the reflection of our soul cannot be seen properly and nothing of the inner or spiritual world can be seen. Attachment towards the material world is the dirt of the mind. The dirt of the mind is very harmful for *Kriya* practitioners so while the dirt of the mind exists, we cannot move even a single inch towards the path of God.

Only by getting rid of all the sins can we progress and have no attachment towards anything in the spiritual world. Then we will have no obstacles on our *kriya* path and materialistic happiness, or sorrow can never affect our mind.

The power to suppress the materialistic thoughts is called yoga. By concentrating our mind on *ajna chakra* when we do *kriya*, all our channels filled with air, breathing becomes very slow without any restlessness, without any concern, without any uneasiness, then the mind leaves its connection with all five *chakras* and stabilizes in *ajna chakra*.

In the beginning of *kriya* practice, no one can do perfect *pranayam*. By after a long practice of following the *guru*'s instructions, we will be able to do perfect *pranayam*; then, by continuous practice of this perfect *pranayam,* we will gradually be able to reach the stage of perfect *uttam pranayam*. *Kriya* in all six *chakras* is done by *uttam pranayam* only.

The *pranayam* we start with in the beginning of *kriya* practice leads to *uttam pranayam*. After that the entire yogic process of piercing the six *chakras* is done by *uttam pranayam*. By practicing *uttam pranayam* both our mind and *prana* (life force) get stillness. Thus, mind as well as *prana* become fixed in *ajna chakra*.

# Questions from Practitioners

**A devotee asked: "I've been practicing *kriya* for a while, but recently I have begun to worry that I am not making enough progress."**

This worry is the result of your expectations. Don't worry. Just go on practicing. Then, I guarantee hundred percent that you will experience the effects of *kriya*. It is difficult to say when this will happen for you. Each of us has different karma that affects the timing of when the effects of *kriya* will become noticeable.

Let the time for that come on its own. All of a sudden, it will happen. It may happen at night when you practice, or it may happen in the day. You don't know when. Every time you do *kriya*, practice it without expectations. Perfect *pranayam* is required. One day you will see what happens. Just carry on without looking left and right.

**Some other *kriya* lineages practice techniques like *Navi Kriya*, *Kechari Mudra*. Why don't we practice those techniques in this lineage?**

I went to my *Guru* with the same question. He asked me, "Why do you want to complicate your life?" He explained to me that these techniques are not necessary and that everything can be achieved through the first *kriya*. It was only later on that Swami Vivekananda heard about the technique of *Kechari Mudra*; he made all progress without it.

**"I have been trying to prolong *Yoni Mudra* by forcibly holding the breath, but now find it difficult to hold my breath for the same length of time as I did previously. What should I do?"**

First, no one can get God by force. It takes complete surrender. Trying to force things comes from expectations. The other name of expectations is desire. We should not have any expectations, even in *kriya*. Only then will we attain real success. Also, we must always be careful not to injure ourselves whether we are practicing a *kriya* technique or even just sitting in an *asana*.

Once your breath lengthens and you reach the stage of *uttam pranayam*, where breath air is not felt outside the nostrils, then you use mental force in *pranayam* after piercing the *sushumna* until the lower part of *ajna chakra*.

**Sometimes it happens when I am practicing the 108 *pranayams* that I stop and seem to go into *paravasta*. Is this all right? Or, and when, should I continue with the *pranayam*?**

Your mind is starting to get fixed at the *ajna chakra*. Very good. You are experiencing a calmness and stillness. That is the goal. If you come back from that state after a little while to your practice of *pranayam*, then your fingers will be where you left off in the count. That will be helpful; because, otherwise, you will not be able to understand or to remember your place. At that point you continue with the *pranayam* unless you are already much deeper.

It is important to know the precise degree of your calmness. If you continue in deep calmness for a long time, then, then you don't have to continue with the *pranayam*. Remaining in deep calmness for a long time means that you have moved from the restless stage of *pranayam* to a calm stage. That can happen, but one should not think too early that he has already reached that stage. In real calmness, everything stops, your mind, your breathing ... eventually you are in *samadhi*.

**What if I am not yet a vegetarian, should I just stop eating meat abruptly?**

Some people are able to become a vegetarian without difficulty; others may need a little time; and still others will need to approach the task more carefully. It depends on your body, your past habits, and attachment to meat.

Ceasing immediately and abruptly a habit to which one is firmly attached in support of one's *sadhana* (for spiritual reasons) can occasionally have an opposite effect to the desired result.

A frontal approach to confronting the ego is not always successful. Instead, for some it will be better to ease off gradually from the habit until one can relinquish (let go of) the desire to eat meat, eggs, etc. One does this by partaking just a little without making it a feast, then stopping at that point thereby satisfying the mind, and in this way gradually weaning oneself off meat and eggs.

**What if I have a history of indulging in sex and still want to practice *Kriya*?**

First, and it goes without saying, that no one cannot make spiritual progress when the mind is restless and externalized in the material world. That's the first thing.

People come to the practice of *Kriya* from many lives with different *vasanas* (latent tendencies) and *samskaras* (mental impressions).

If the viewing of mental images is involved, try not to watch or engage in mental images about activities that you want to curtail, as mental images and sounds merge together in kind of a trance, and become even more powerful than either one is alone in impressing themselves on your consciousness.

Another way to overcome this is, rather than taking a major egoic stand against such activity, you might consider telling yourself firmly, "not now" or "not at this time." As a result, you are not telling yourself you will never engage in the activity you want to curtail, just that you will not engage in it at this time. Then, whenever the desire reappears again, repeat the same thing to yourself. "Not today, not at this time." That way you are living increasingly in the present. You can use the same method to curtail a variety of behaviors that you want to eliminate.

Real success comes when the desire no long arises, but the karmic seeds can take a long time to disappear. This is where cleaning the *nadis* through *pranayam* can be so helpful as eventually the seeds will be extinguished.

Regardless of what your past experience, don't allow any guilt or shame about any of your activities to separate you from God. God doesn't care about your sins, but when you continue to repeat them, it will keep you from experiencing the Divine.

After *kriya* initiation, it is not possible, for a practitioner to completely control the urge for sex. Since you are not able at this stage to stop the urge right away, and to overcome the desire completely, you should reasonably seek to moderate it. With the practice of *kriya*, the desire for sex will gradually diminish as your calmness deepens, but the important thing is this: you still have to make the effort. As much as possible, one has to avoid always thinking of sex, and to avoid bad films, and all those things that are harmful to your kriya---wrong thinking, wrong seeing, and wrong hearing.

*Kriya Yoga* is not just about meditation and practicing *pranayam,* and the other techniques, given in initiation. It is also involves controlling the mind. The mind can be our best friend or our worse enemy. Without controlling and calming the mind down, however, no further development will take place.

It is not until, and unless, one has pierced the *manipura chakra* that one has control over the sex urge. Up until that point, *raja guna* is present. *Raja guna* means that the restlessness of mind is present. This is why eating the right foods is so important, as wrong foods make the mind restless. In deep meditation, you cannot think of sex, the mind is so calm so strive for to attain that calmness in your practice.

**Sometimes I notice that other devotees are making more progress than I am. What can do?**

Most people who take *kriya* initiation, and start the practice of *Kriya Yoga,* still have to perform many duties with their families, at work, and in society. As a result, in the beginning they don't necessarily have a lot of time to practice *kriya*.

Practice the best you can for where you are at this stage in your spiritual life. Be earnest. Practice *kriya* persistently and with patience. Just as you do certain things every day like eating and sleeping, you practice *kriya*.

In the beginning, that is enough, but please, understand, you still have to make the effort. This does not give you a "free pass" to relax your vigil. Everyone has to struggle against bad habits. As you advance, you will do more.

Regarding your comparison with others, why compare yourself with someone else when what you are seeking is within? Win or lose is the strategy of the ego. Comparisons with others just strengthen the ego. Whatever other devotees are doing, what is that to you? You don't know your own karma or anyone else's. Let go of your expectations and just focus on your own practice.

**"Why is the food we eat so important in *kriya*?"**

After starting a *kriya* practice, at first one may not realize how important it is to eat the proper foods. We all know, of course, that eating the wrong foods can disturb our peace, calmness, digestion, practice of *pranayam* and mediation, and even our sleep.

As you start to regulate your life and to control the senses, you discover that one wrong action like eating spicy food can cause indigestion which next disturbs your sleep [so you sleep less]. Then, as a result of a lack of sleep, you notice your *kriya* practice suffers the next morning. The point is that a wrong action made at one point in time can have adverse consequences that propagate to a later time and can even continue beyond that. The right food and right living (the *yamas* and *niyamas*) are needed to keep our minds calm.

These kinds of misdeeds in daily life, even if they seem small and insignificant, create a chain of events that makes us live, or exist, at the effect of our actions. As a result, like the waves in a storm, we are buffeted by the effects of our actions; and as a result, instead of living free and aware, we live karmically.

The correct practice of *pranayam* by daily cleansing of our nerves through *nadi shuddhi* can correct these and other misdeeds, but when, we continue to commit misdeeds while practicing *kriya*, we are just 'treading water' instead of making progress towards our real goal. The result that we will then have to practice *kriya* for a longer period of time in order to make progress. So, start to make real progress now by right living and by practicing *kriya*.

# A Story about the Kutastha and my Guruji

My father had prostate cancer; and when he was in a very serious condition, my brother-in-law went to my *Guruji* to ask him about my father's condition, wanting to know what would happen. At that point, my *Guruji* told him that he would survive the current crisis at this time, but, he may not the next time. After one year, my father died. Below is the technique my *Guruji* employed.

To employ this technique, <u>one first has to be able to enter the *sushumna* and *Kutastha*</u>. Now, think of a problem. Any of three different results may present themselves: either the problem will have a successful outcome, or it will not have a successful outcome, or the result will come, but at a later time. After you think of the problem, then close your eyes, and while watching the *Kutastha*, take a deep breath and hold your attention there at the *Kutastha*. Then, you will see one of three types of color. If you see a golden yellow color, then the result will be positive (success). If you see a red color, then the result will not be positive (not a success). If you see a gray color, that means success will come later, but not at this time.

# Some Key Points

- Practicing *kriya* on either an empty stomach or on a too full stomach is not good.

- In the beginning *pranayam* is the most important part of *kriya* until we pierce the *ajna chakra*. *Kriya* should be practiced in a very relaxed mind without hurrying to complete it.

- A *kriya* practitioner should eat vegetables, fruits, milk, ghee, etc., and avoid not non-vegetarian items such as eggs, meat, etc.

- Don't waste time repenting for your past deeds. Past is always past. The future is always uncertain. So, think only about the present.

- It is a sin if we don't practice *kriya* after initiation.

- A married person may in the beginning sleep with his wife only twice a month, then gradually one should maintain celibacy.

- For advancement to the higher states, mixing with the opposite sex is strictly prohibited, as temptations and entanglements will bind us, keeping our consciousness centered in the lower centers.

- Always try to sleep alone in bed.

- A *Kriya* practitioner should sometimes stay alone to practice in some remote place.

- We should not make our mind more restless by thinking, why our mind is not getting calmness. If we practice according to the instructions, calmness is bound to come.

- Sex, anger, desire always happen to the restless mind. When mind becomes calm, desires will disappear.

- In the beginning the mind will try to disturb us very much, but with practice, gradually and slowly, the mind will become calm.

- No one will can progress in *kriya* without chanting OM.

- By practicing *kriya*, the inner world will become lit.

- Mind cannot be calm without doing *kriya*; and when mind becomes very calm, meditation starts. Calming and controlling the mind is very important in *Kriya Yoga*. That is why in first and second *kriya*, the most important thing to practice perfect *pranayam*.

- One can be free of sins, if he or she practices *kriya* perfectly.

- Always practice *kriya* without expectations.

- After piercing the *anahata chakra*, the force that one places on *pranayam* becomes less.

- Practicing *kriya* without initiation and opening of the third eye is fruitless.

- Always practice *kriya* keeping the spinal cord straight.

- Intoxication happens after practicing *kriya* for a long time.

- *Guru kripa* (grace of Guru) comes automatically if a *kriya* practitioner follows correct procedure.

- Always keep in mind, if you get salvation, that is OK; and even if you don't get salvation in this life, it is also OK. Ultimately, even the desire for salvation is a desire that must be renounced. Let *Kriya* take us to the gate of salvation and then see what happens.

- Generally, a serious and good *kriya* practitioner will gain salvation in one or two lifetimes. Knowing that can reassure us, but we still have to practice with discipline sincerely.

- With first *kriya*, we may get everything.

- By practicing perfect *pranayam*, we will get peace of mind.

- Always remain alert whether or not you are doing perfect *pranayam*. Awareness is important. The mind should always be alert.

- We have to practice *kriya* every day, at the same place, in the same *asana* at the same time, and with the same number of *pranayams* in order to experience the joy and benefits of *kriya*.

- By practicing *Kriya Yoga*, *kundalini* power gets quickly activated.

- To advance faster and get stillness sooner, we have to practice *kriya* at least three times a day.

- At the point between the eyebrows, one can perceive the *sushumna*. Whatever object you see, watch it at the center. This is the wisdom that I received from my *Guruji*. So, always watch the center, otherwise, you will miss it.

- At the time of death (last breath) we see either white light or total darkness. By watching the white light, when we leave our body, then it is as good as *moksha*. If we are engulfed in darkness, we have to take birth again and again.

Made in the USA
Las Vegas, NV
22 March 2025

19977725R00042